MAGIC EYE

A New Way of Looking at the World

3D Illusions by N.E. Thing Enterprises

Andrews and McMeel
A Universal Press Syndicate Company
Kansas City

ISBN: 0-8362-7006-1

"Children" photo, page 10, © Melanie Carr. Courtesy of Southern Stock Uniphoto Press International.

First Printing, September 1993
Second Printing, November 1993
Third Printing, December 1993
Fourth Printing, January 1994
Fifth Printing, January 1994
Sixth Printing, January 1994
Seventh Printing, January 1994

─── ATTENTION: SCHOOLS AND BUSINESSES ───

Andrews and McMeel books are available at quantity discounts with bulk purchase for educational, business, or sales promotional use. For information, please write to: Special Sales Department, Andrews and McMeel, 4900 Main Street, Kansas City, Missouri 64112.

INTRODUCTION

So, what is a MAGIC EYE picture? How does it work? Most importantly, how can you learn to "see" it too?

MAGIC EYE is the method of viewing a unique 3D picture that can be printed on plain paper with no special coatings, and viewed without special glasses. The basic idea has been around for many years. Some people call early variations of MAGIC EYE pictures Single Image Random Dot Stereograms. Some other people do not believe any of this, but that's another story.

During the 1960s, Dr. Bella Julesz was the first to use computer-generated 3D images made up of randomly placed dots to study depth perception in human beings. Because the dot pictures did not contain any other information, like color or shapes, he could be sure that when his subject saw the picture it was 3D only!

In the years that followed, other people continued using random dot pictures in their work; many of them were graduate students who studied with Dr. Julesz. With time they found new and better ways to create their interesting illusions.

In recent years, hobbyists and artists have advanced this amazing technique. They not only saw that further technical innovation was possible based on the basic random dot technique, but also that an entirely new art form might be possible. As in the field of fractals, powerful home computers have made both art and science based on extensive computations available to anyone who had the energy to explore these new frontiers. One notable person who has ventured into this area is Dan Dyckman, whose various entertainments and articles have enriched many of us. Another is Mike Bielinski, whose various art and technical products have vastly broadened the awareness and appreciation of STARE-E-O 3D imaging.

We, at N.E. Thing Enterprises, have worked for the past years with our partner company in Japan, Tenyo Co. Ltd. In Japan, STARE-E-O images and MAGIC EYE books have skyrocketed into a major cultural phenomenon. More than 750,000 MAGIC EYE books sold there in a period of eight months, spanning 1992 and 1993; 200,000 copies were sold in Korea during the first month of publication! In addition, over a dozen competing books have been published, with many unique, beautiful, and interesting images created by a growing worldwide community of 3D artists!

In Japan, 3D image viewing has been the subject of many TV talk and quiz shows. Some shops selling 3D goods even report a flourishing "dating scene" as the experienced offer to share their vast knowledge with an attractive, but inexperienced, newcomer. It's a great opportunity for one-liners, such as, "Gosh, you look so sweet with your eyes crossed!" or "You should see the 3D pattern on my carpet at home."

For us, it has been a wild ride, much of it with a cyberspace sense of barely virtual reality. Like many magical experiences, it soon took over those of us who naively "rubbed the lantern." So, prepare yourself. Once you discover and train your MAGIC EYE, you'll never doubt that no matter what you think you see, there's more to be revealed.

VIEWING TECHNIQUES

Learning to use your MAGIC EYE is a bit like learning to ride a bicycle. Once you get it, it gets easier and easier. If possible, try to learn to use your MAGIC EYE in a quiet, meditative time and place. It is difficult for most people to first experience deep vision while otherwise preoccupied in the distracting pinball machine of life. While others teach you, or watch as you try, you're likely to feel foolish and suffer from performance anxiety. Although MAGIC EYE is great fun at work and other entertaining social situations, those are not often the best places to learn. If you don't get it in two or three minutes, wait until another, quieter time. And, if it's hard for you, remember, the brain fairy did not skip your pillow. For most people, it's a real effort to figure out how to use the MAGIC EYE. Almost all of them tell us the effort was well worth it!

In all of the images in MAGIC EYE, you'll note a repeating pattern. In order to "see" a MAGIC EYE picture, two things must happen. First, you must get *one* eye to look at a point in the image, while the *other* eye looks at the same point in the next pattern. Second, you must hold your eyes in that position long enough for the marvelous structures in your brain to decode the 3D information that has been coded into the repeating patterns by our computer programs.

There are two methods of viewing our 3D images: Crossing your eyes and diverging your eyes. Crossing your eyes occurs when you aim your eyes at a point between your eyes and an image; diverging your eyes occurs when your eyes are aimed at a point beyond the image.

All of our pictures are designed to be seen by diverging the eyes. It is also possible to see them with the cross-eyed method, but all the depth information comes out backward! (If you try it, we *can* guarantee that *you* will not come backward, too.) If we intend to show an airplane flying in front of a cloud, using the diverging eye method, you will see an airplane-shaped hole cut into the cloud if you look at it with the cross-eyed method. Once you learn one method, try the other. It's fun, but most people do better with one or the other. We think that most people prefer the diverging method.

Another common occurrence is to diverge the eyes twice as far as is needed to see the image. In this case, a weird, more complex version of the intended object is seen. (By the way, if you diverge your eyes while looking at yourself in a mirror, you can find your "third eye" . . . at least we were told that in a letter we received. But you must spend several hours a day looking at yourself in a mirror. Remember, we said it was all right.)

One last note before you start. Although this technique is safe, and even potentially helpful to your eyes, don't overdo it! Straining will not help, and could cause you to feel uncomfortable. That is not the way to proceed. Ask your nephew or the paper girl to give you some help; they'll probably be able to do it in ten seconds. The key is to relax and let the image come to you.

METHOD ONE

Hold the image so that it touches your nose. (Ignore those who might be tempted to make comments about you.) Let the eyes relax, and stare vacantly off into space, as if looking through the image. Relax and become comfortable with the idea of observing the image, without looking *at* it. When you are relaxed and not crossing your eyes, move the page *slowly* away from your face. Perhaps an inch every two or three seconds. Keep looking through the page. Stop at a comfortable reading distance and keep staring. The most discipline is needed when something starts to "come in," because at that moment you'll instinctively try to look *at* the page rather than looking through it. If you look *at* it, *start again.*

METHOD TWO

The cover of this book is shiny; hold it in such a way that you can identify a reflection. For example, hold it under an overhead lamp so that it catches its light. Simply look at the object you see reflected, and continue to stare at it with a fixed gaze. After several seconds, you'll perceive depth, followed by the 3D image, which will develop almost like an instant photo!

The images in this book are of increasing difficulty. The last pages provide a key that shows the 3D picture which you'll see when you find and train your MAGIC EYE.

The first three images in the book do not contain a hidden picture; instead the various repeated objects will seem to float in space at different distances when viewed correctly. For many, they are easier to see than the other pictures.

We wish you luck, and hope you enjoy this fantastic new art form!

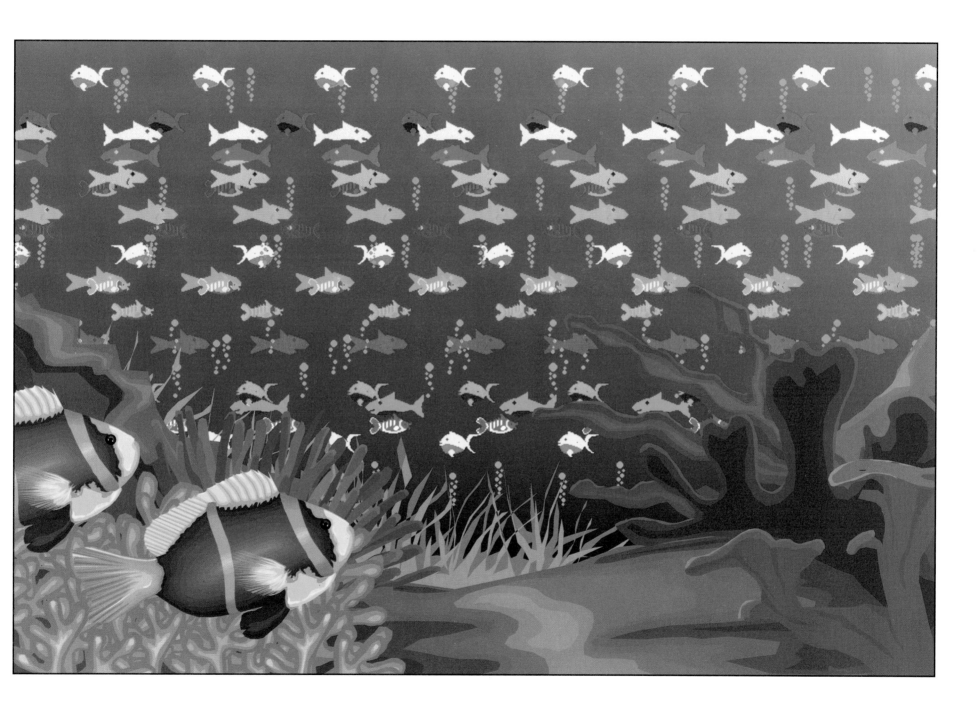

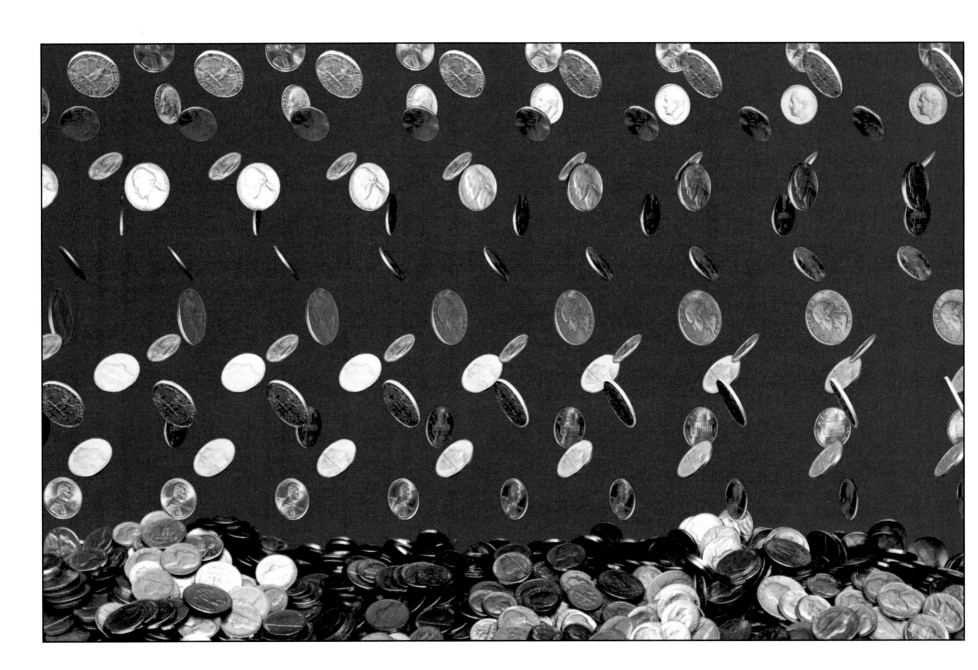

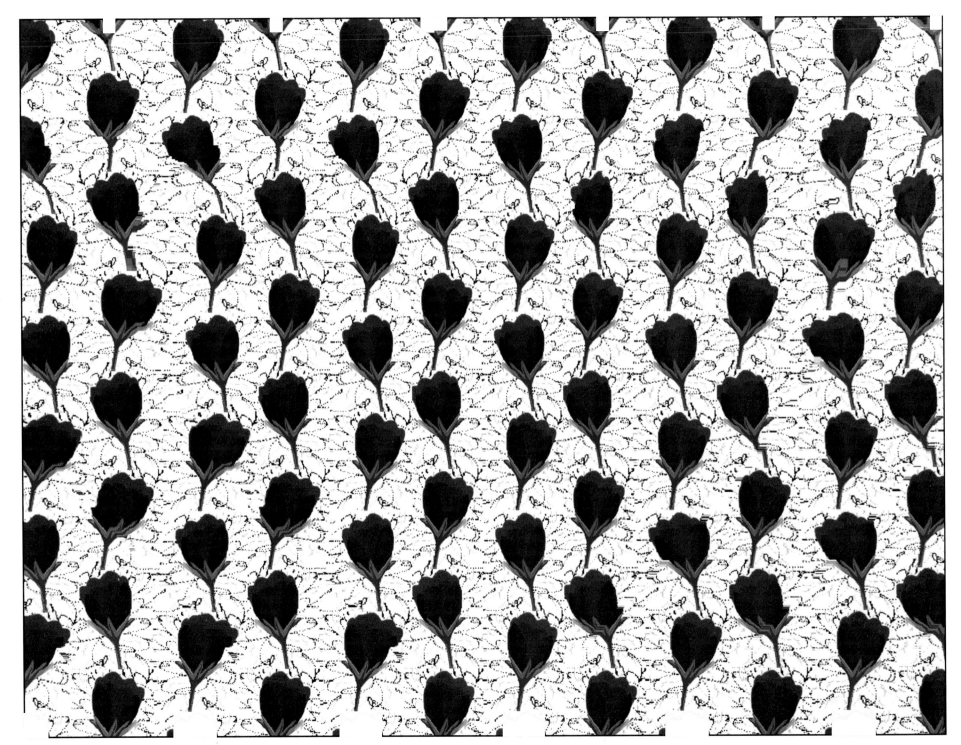

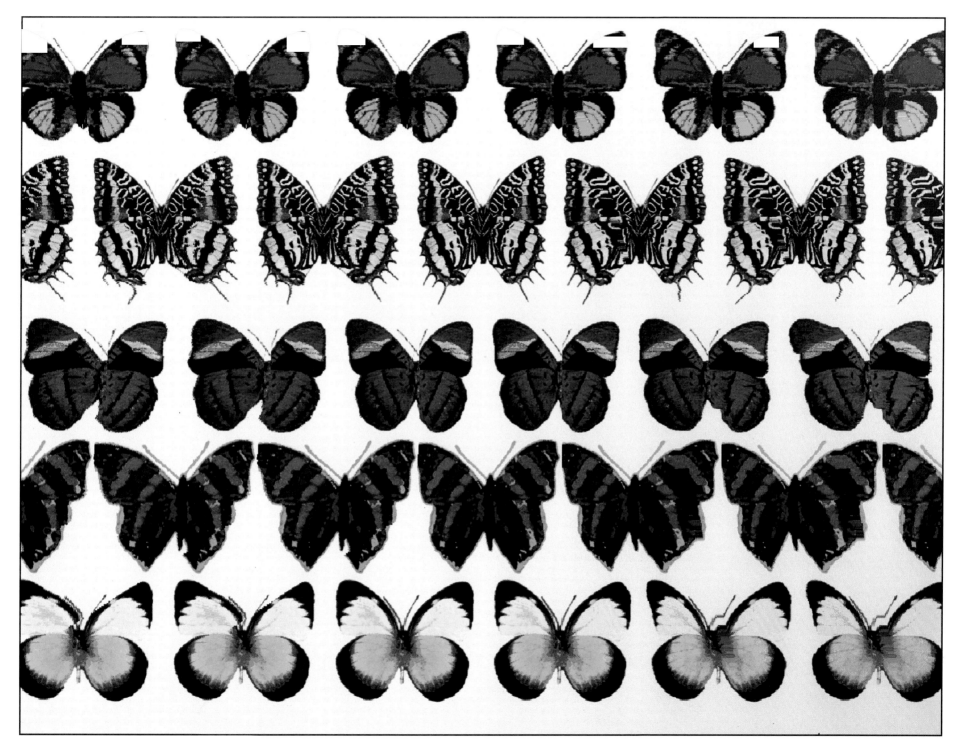

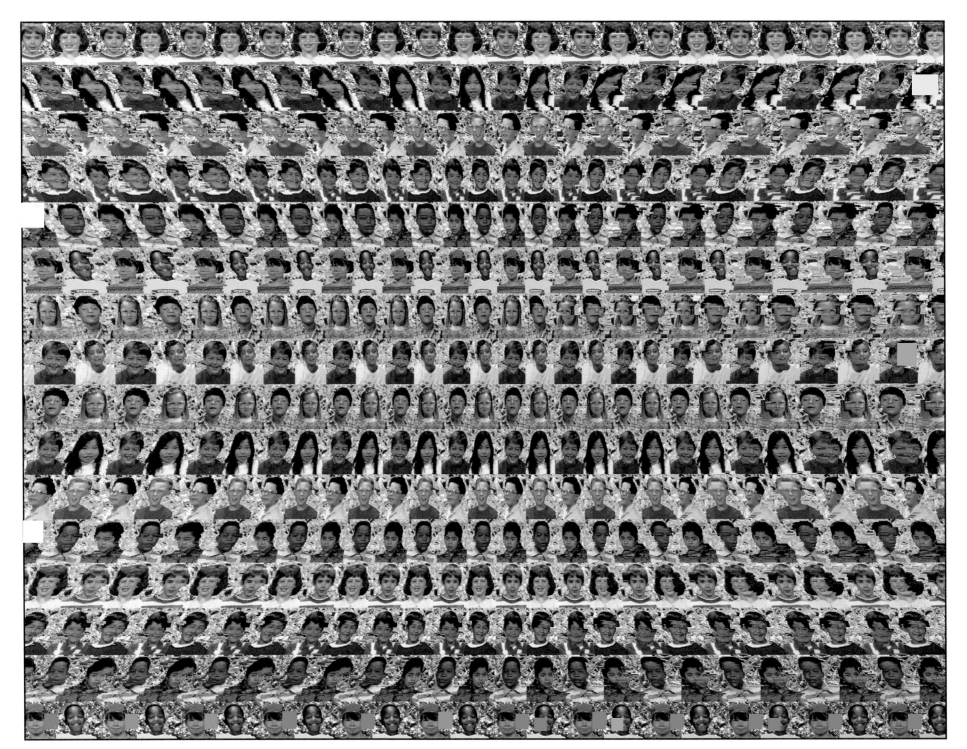

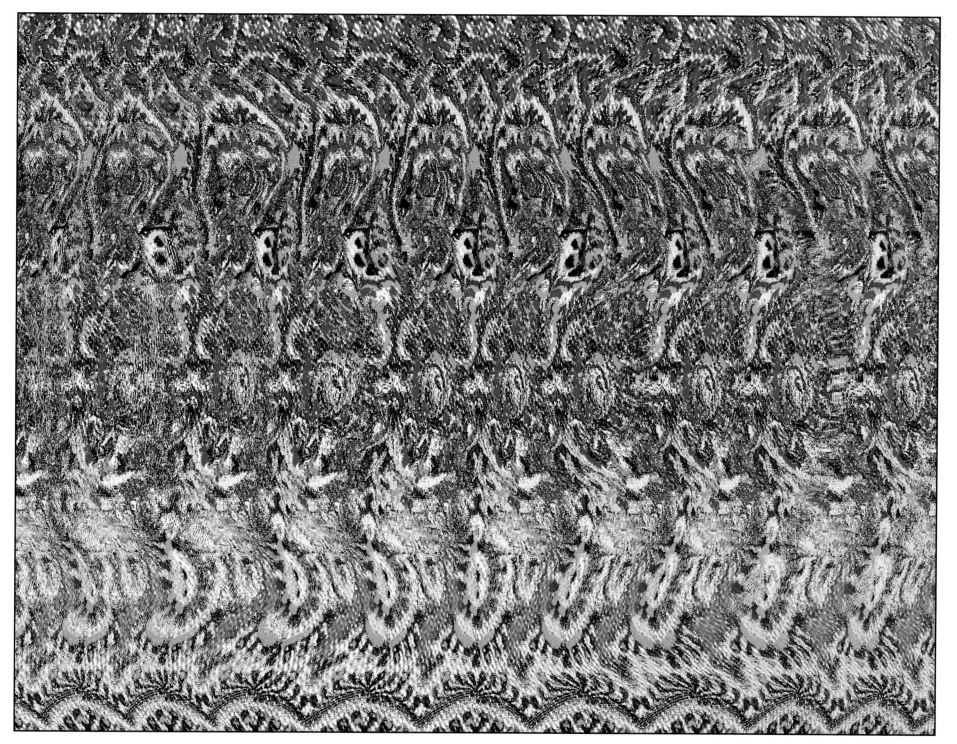

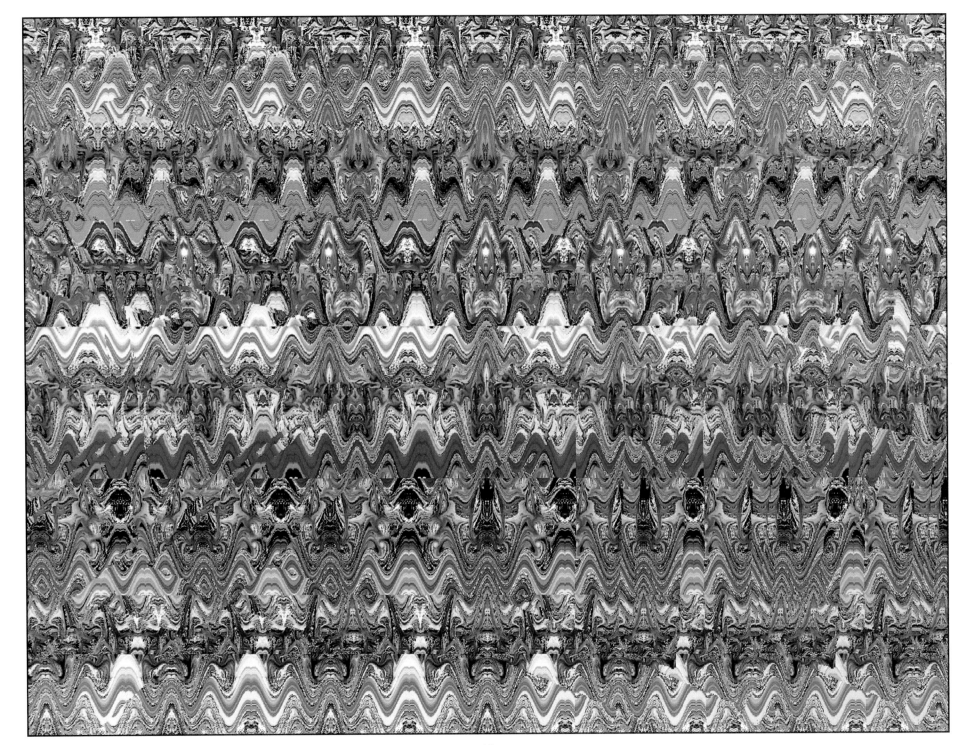

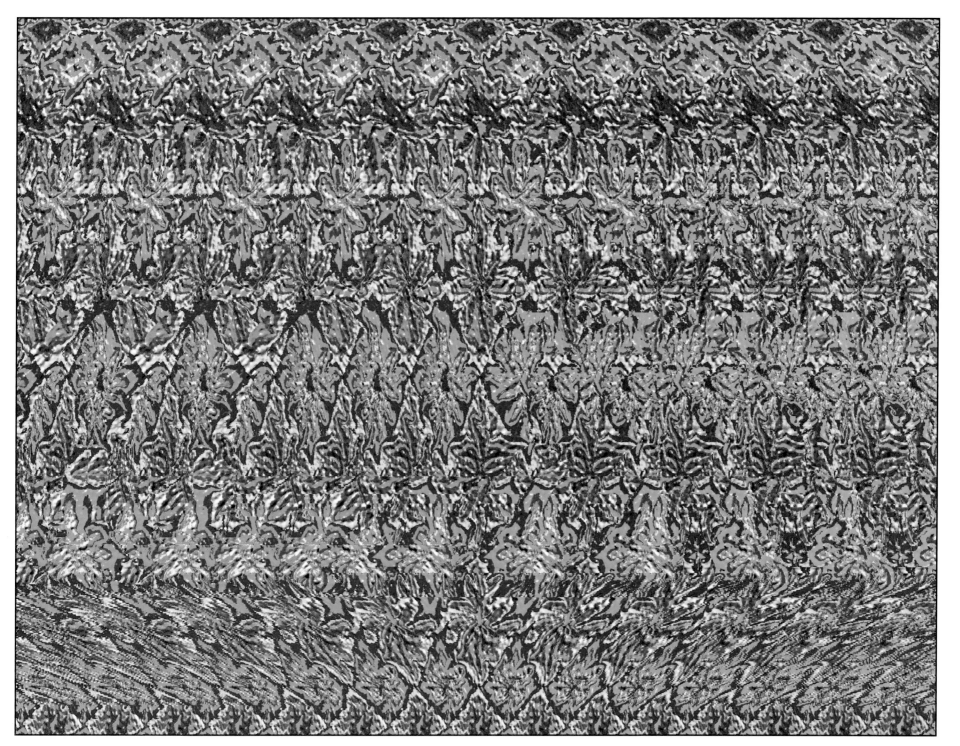

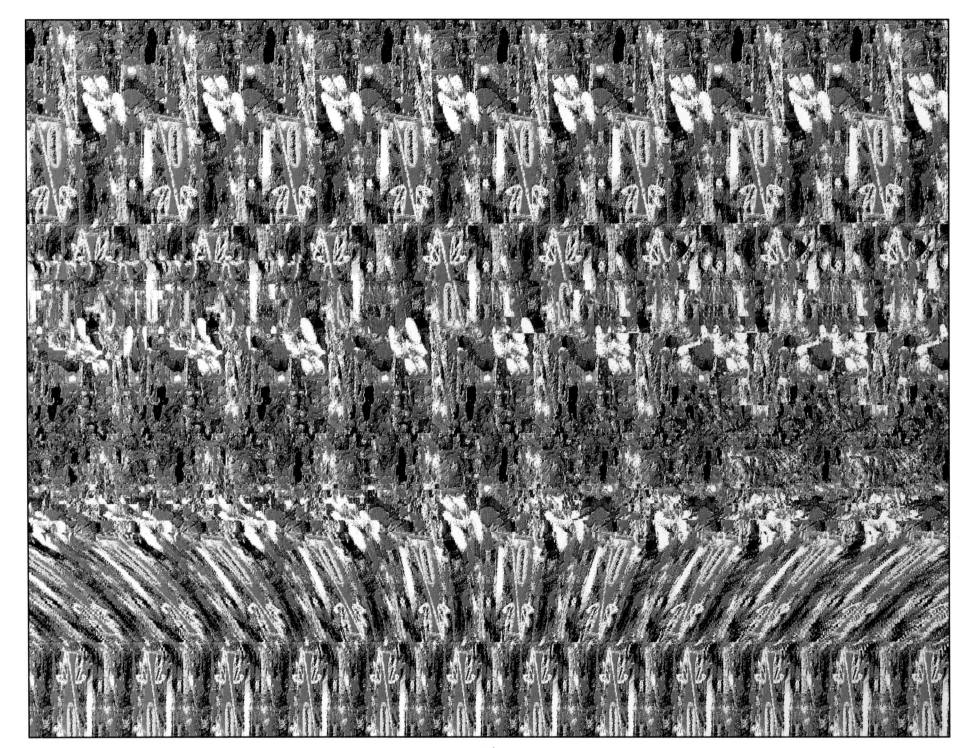

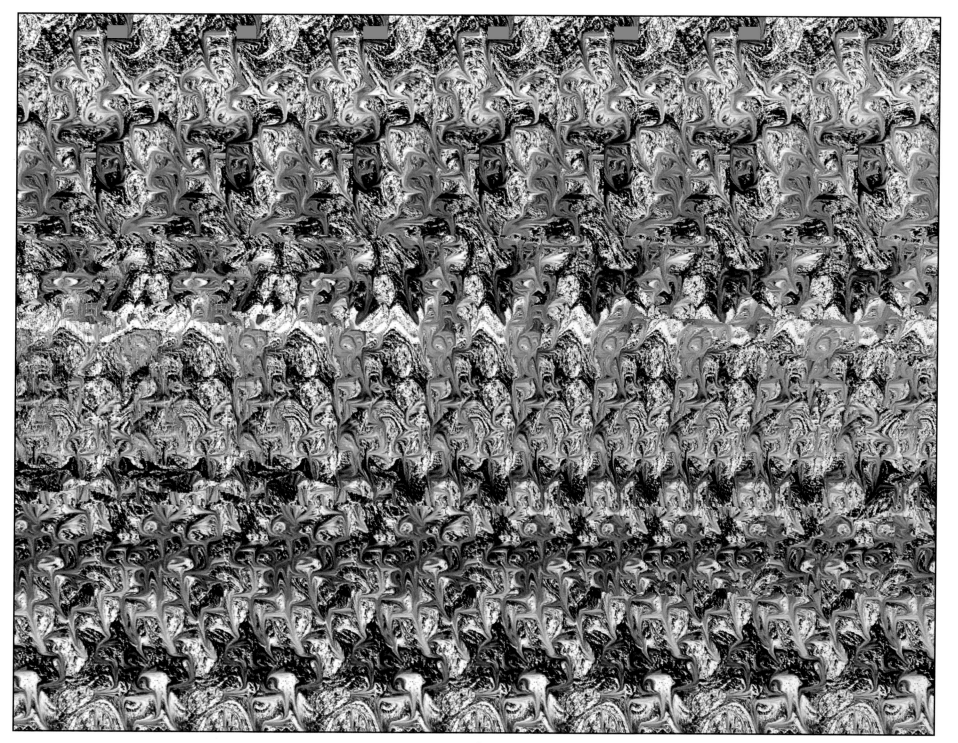

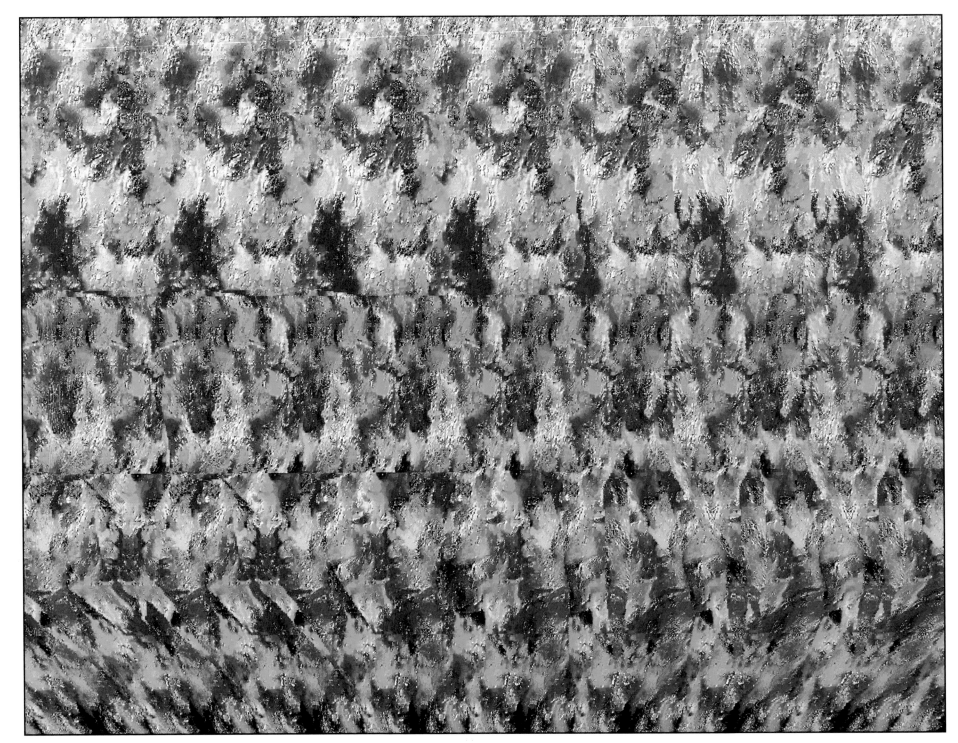

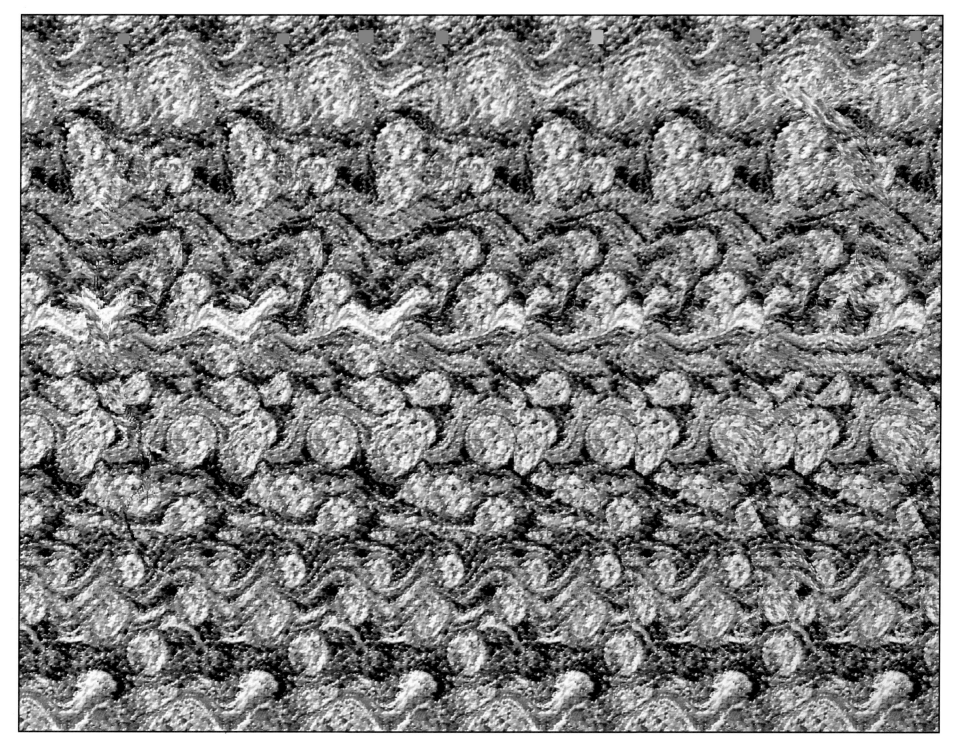

17

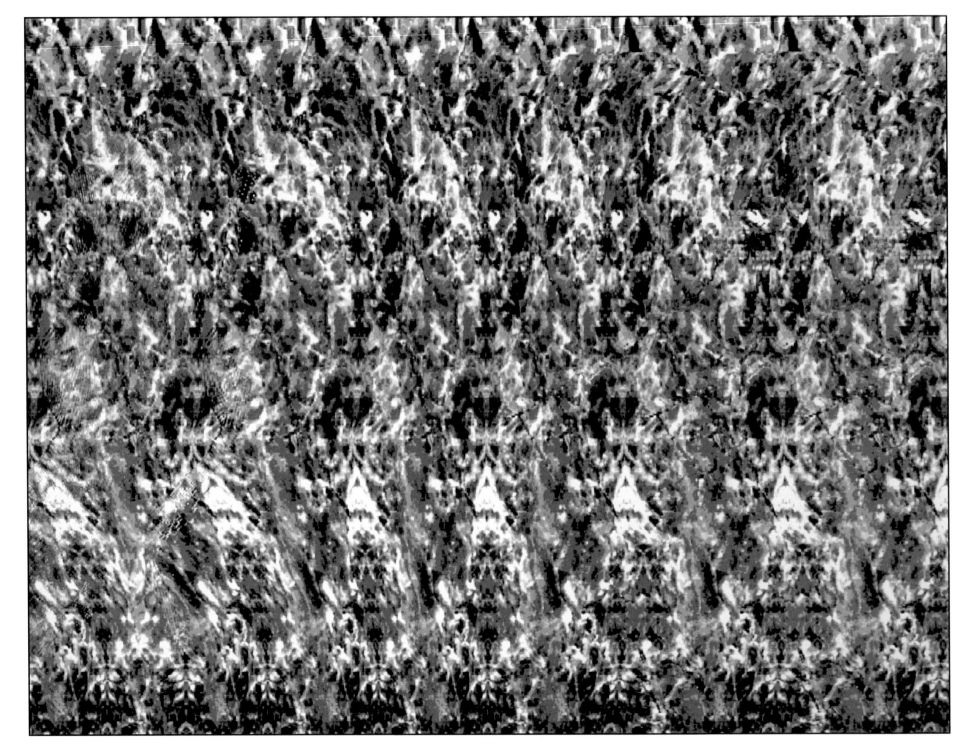

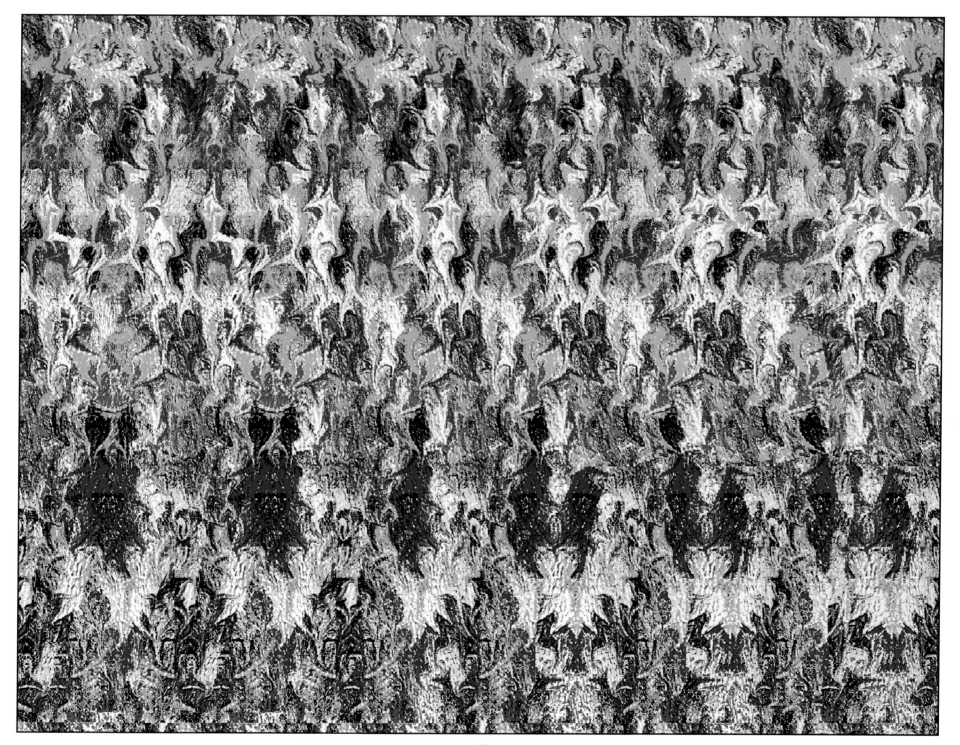

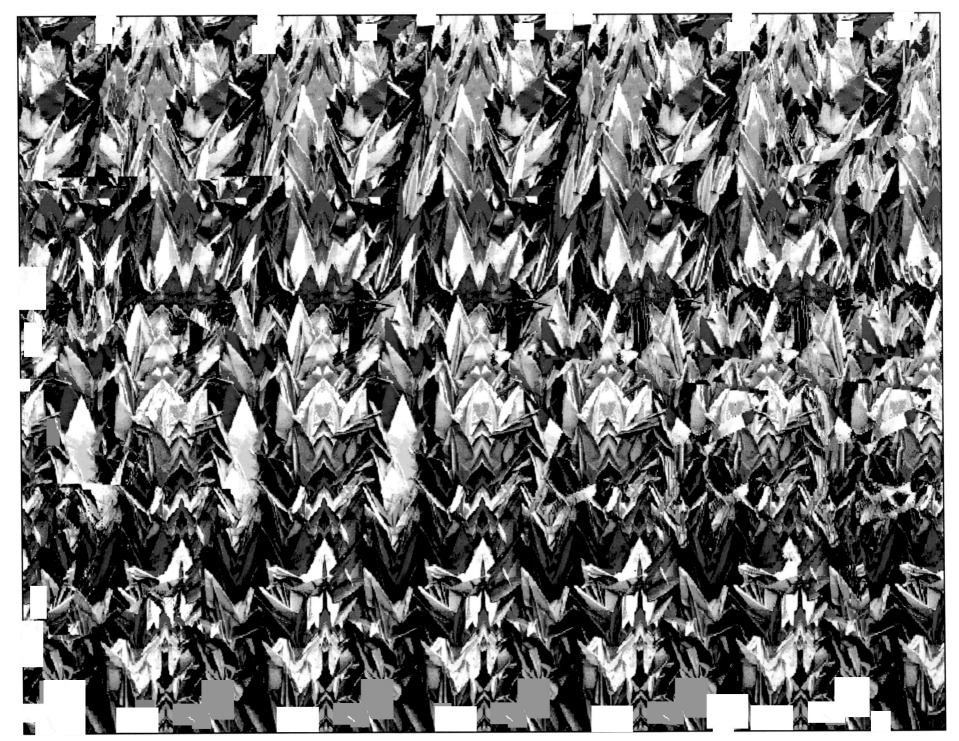

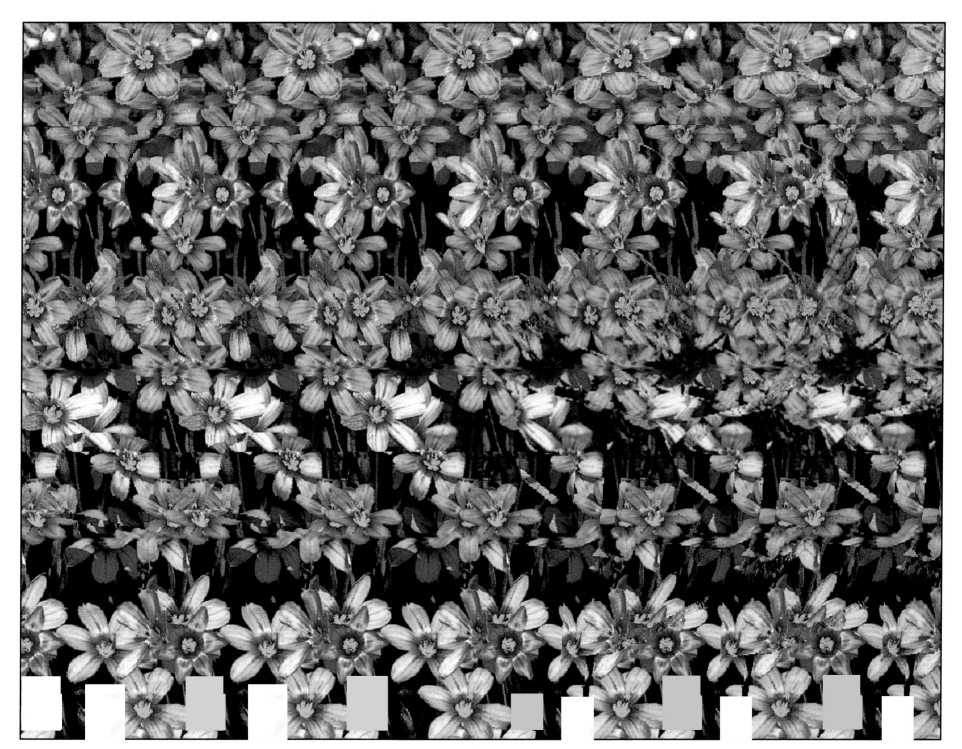

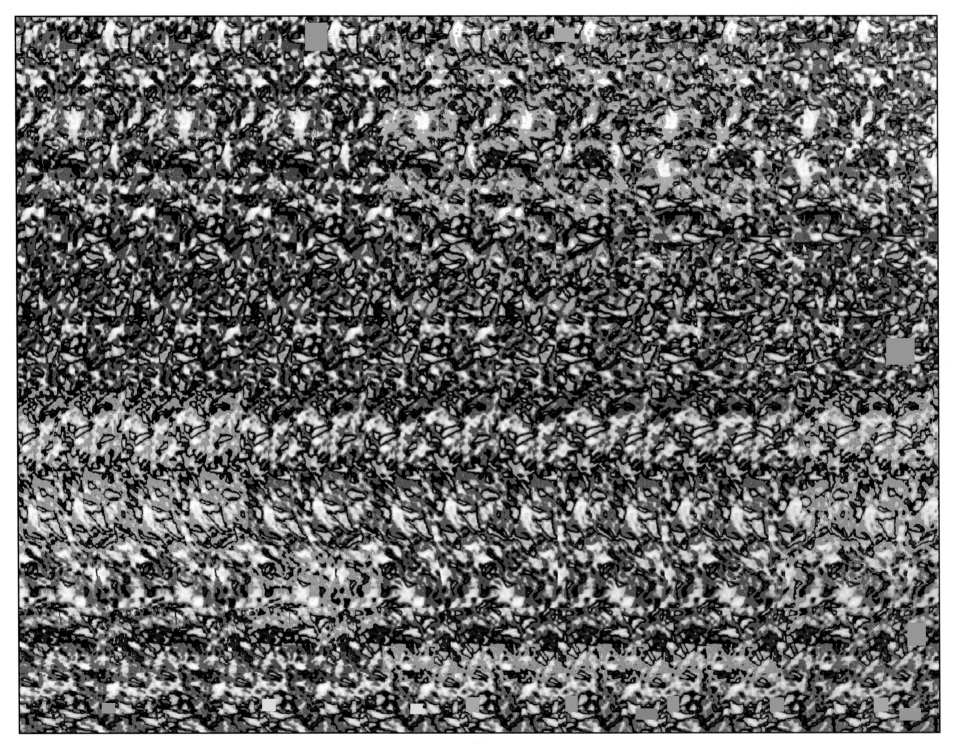

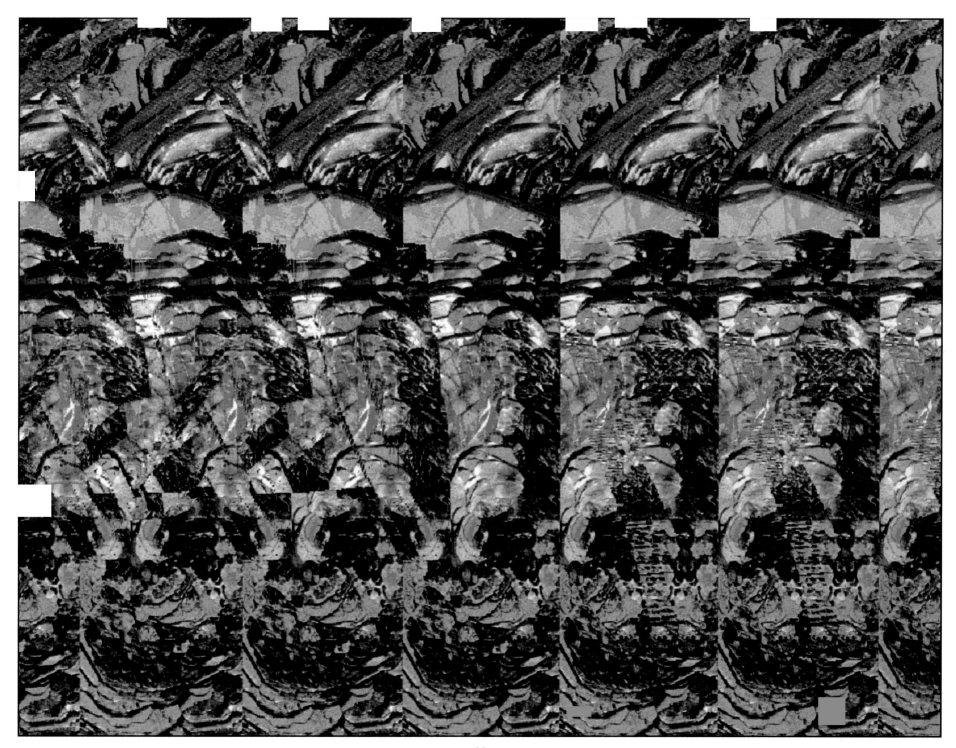

23

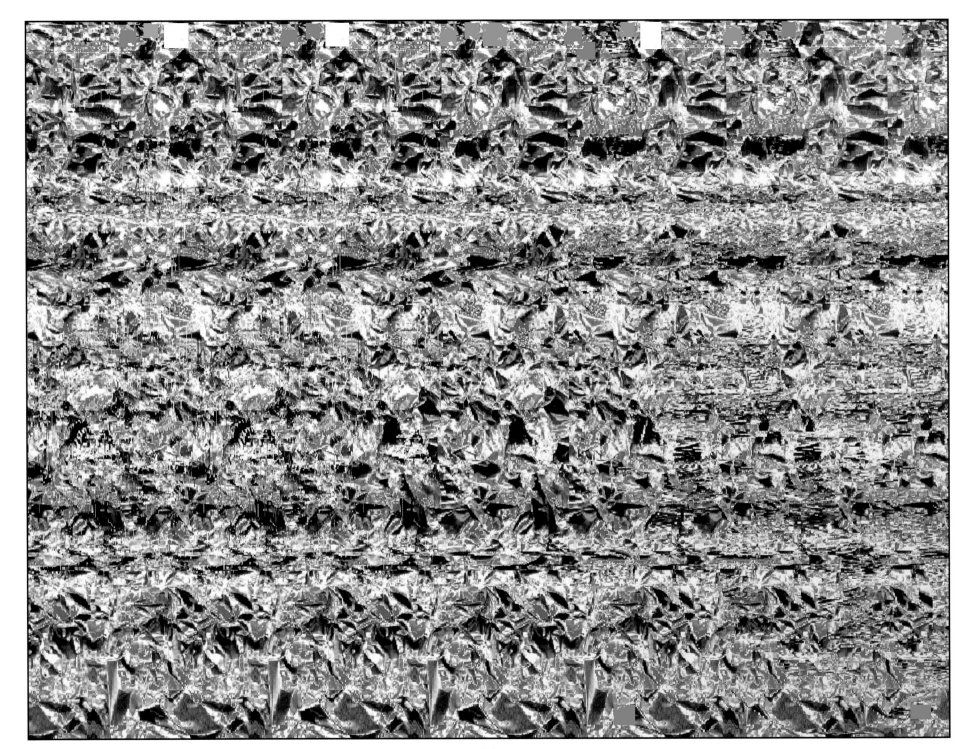

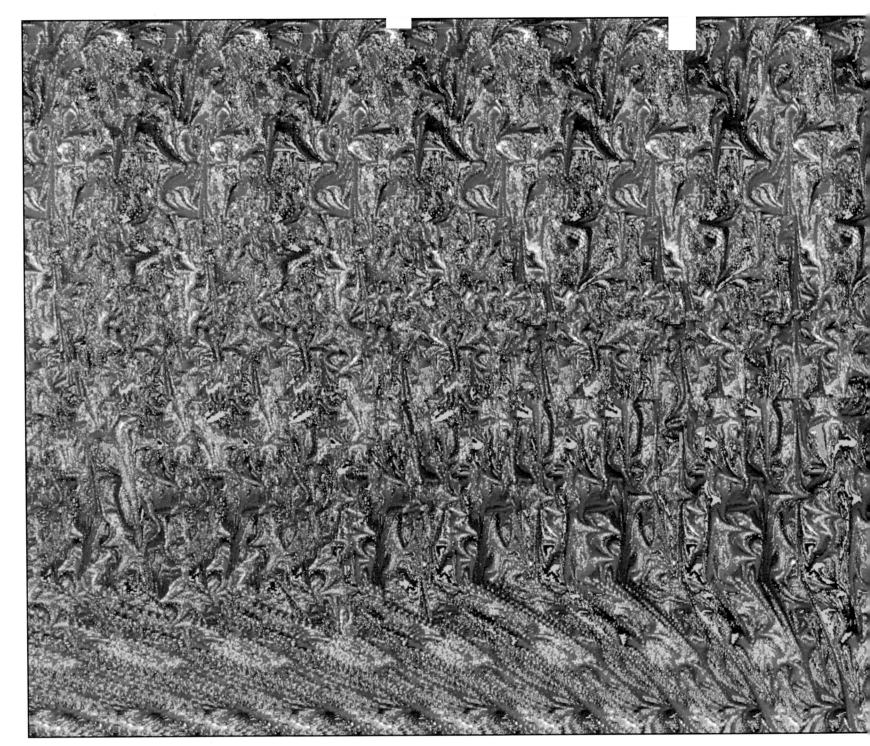

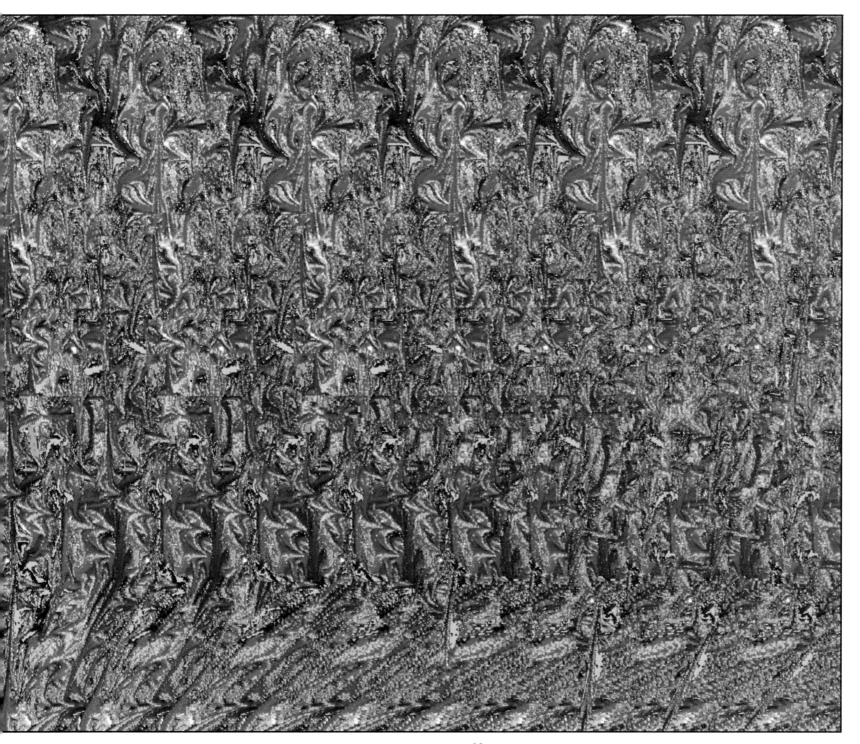

Page 8 Heart

Page 9 Star

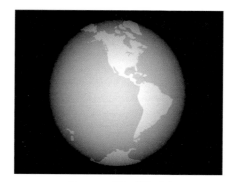

Page 10 The World

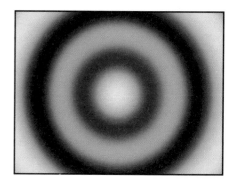

Page 11 Raindrop

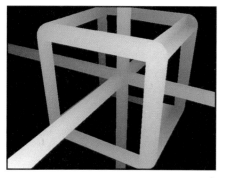

Page 12 Cube

Page 13 Boxing Kangaroos

Page 14 Train

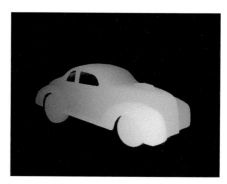

Page 15 Hot Rod

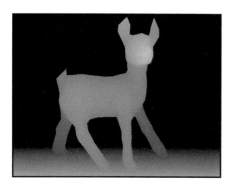

Page 16 Deer

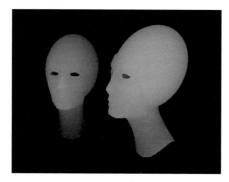

Page 17 Aliens

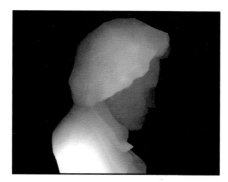

Page 18 Ludwig van Beethoven

Page 19 Lamb

Page 20 Paper Stars

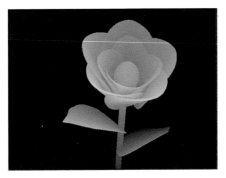

Page 21 Flower

Page 22 Still Life

Page 23 X29 / Fighter Plane

Page 24 Motor Bike

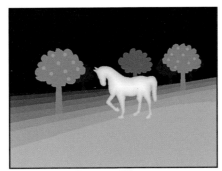

Page 25 Horse

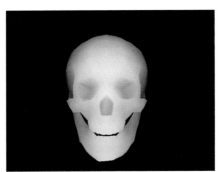

Page 26 Skull

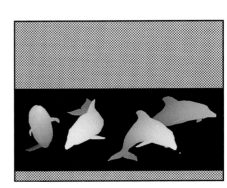

Page 27 Dolphins

Page 28–29 Dinosaurs

Page 30 Crystal Ball